T0151306

The
Philippines
a visual journey

Welcome to the Philippines,
an Archipelago of Enchanted Islands

TUTTLE Publishing

Tokyo | Rutland, Vermont | Singapore

The Philippines

a visual journey

THE PHILIPPINES is a Southeast Asian archipelago of over 7,000 islands strewn between the Pacific Ocean and the Asian mainland. Here Orient meets Occident with a distinctive flair. Three centuries of Spanish Christianization and 40 years of American colonization have left their mark, contributing to the East-West character of a vibrant, Latinized people of Asian bloodlines. Catholicism is the major religion, English is the tongue of the educated, and the soulful creativity of the Filipinos prevails in visual arts and daily life. Music, basketball, boxing and politics are the national pasttimes, from bustling Metro Manila to historic Cebu to booming Davao in Mindanao. Ecotourism adventures await in all 81 provinces—from Boracay to Bohol, Panay to Palawan, to the Banaue Rice Terraces of Northern Luzon. All in this high-spirited place, the Philippines.

Contents

32

52

2

36

55

24

40

59

29

45

62

30

49

64

mabuhay!

WELCOME to one unique Filipino national sensibility—hospitality. Unlike any other Asian nation, the Philippines is a destination readily accessible to visitors from both East and West. Warmth and accommodation come naturally to the islander Filipinos. Guests are feted, honored and shown the best of the country's offerings.

The Philippines can be an exciting, even flamboyant place, driven by the exuberant spirit of the Filipino people. Their hybrid culture derives from a unique mingling of Eastern and Western influences, from diverse Malay, Chinese, Spanish and American strains and bloodlines. Their special character was formed by "four centuries in the convent and four decades in Hollywood," wrote historian Carmen Guerrero Nakpil. However one sees it, Filipinos have evolved a real cosmopolitan flair, topped by their national knack for song, dance and theater throughout seven regions. Welcome to the Philippine Islands' abundance of natural attractions and rich archipelagic experiences beyond the urban centers.

Below: Yellow daisy flower teenagers, about to join the street parade at the Panagbenga Flower Festival in Baguio.

Facing page: Life is a beach on Boracay, one of the top destinations in the Philippines.

4

Mabuhay is the *aloha* greeting of the Philippines. In one word, Mabuhay hails: welcome, farewell and long-live. Spirited Filipinos are among the most hospitable people in the world.

Left: A tricycle driver enjoys a laugh in Divisoria Market, Manila's largest street market.
Right: Cone-shaped Mt Mayon, the main attraction and active volcano of Bicol.
Middle, left: Fresh catch of the day, served on Isla Naburot, Iloilo.
Middle, right: Civic parade passing the heavyset Basilica of Taal, Batangas.
Bottom: Surfboards at sunset on the northern Ilocos coast of the big island, Luzon.

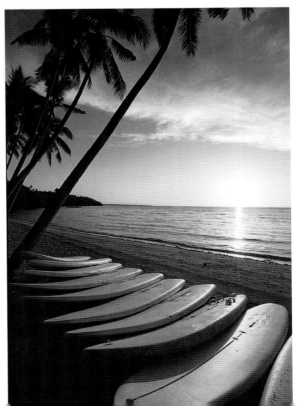

OVER THE CENTURIES, both Spain and America have colonized this fragmented archipelago and left behind their traces—in staunch Roman Catholicism, the Spanish attitude of *mañana* and the American-accented tongue and legislative system. Early Malay-Filipinos intermarried with Chinese and Arabs from the 10th century onwards and were colonized by the Spanish from the 16th to the 19th centuries. The Americans arrived in 1898 and occupied the islands for four decades. In 1946, after the devastation of World War II, the Philippines took its place as Asia's first constitutional democracy. In 1986 and 2001, two popular uprisings called People Power ousted bad leaders, renewed the sense of national self and installed the best Filipinos—women—as Presidents!

Above: Everyday street life in the district of Intramuros, which was the seat of government when the Philippines were a part of the Spanish Empire.

Left: Young female students at "Universidad de Manila". The main campus of this public university is at the heart of the city near the LRT Central Terminal.

Facing page, clockwise from left: Blue face paint on a brown-face w ndsurfer; it's just sunblock, the bathing costume of party island Boracay. Exotic Davao beckons with a pretty face. Rice harvest in Bicol, under the gaze of Mt Mayon.

the filipinos

They are natural musicians and Westernized Asians—a combination of dusky Malay and fiery Spanish, with a touch of Chinese and a generous topping of hip, savvy America.

 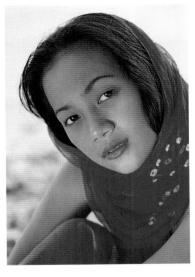

FILIPINOS are playful folks with smiles, easy-going characters and personal kinship systems that keep their world going. Thespian Rolando Tinio said it best: "Like islanders everywhere in the tropics, Filipinos do tend to be quite blissful."

There are two sources of the inner strength and friendliness of the typical Filipino: a fervent belief in the goodness of God, Life and Nature, and a sense of security in and reliance on family ties and neighborhood associations. The typical Filipino is long on religiosity, family, hometown loyalty and cockeyed optimism.

STUDIES ON FILIPINO BEHAVIOR have pointed out distinct values and patterns in Filipino society: *pakikisama* or getting on well with associates; *utang na loob*, which means a deep sense of gratitude for favors received; *hiya* or a strong fear of losing face; and a *bahala na* attitude—things will take care of themselves. Filipinos live in a modern world without being thoroughly modern. The majority are people still in the bosom of Mother Nature—noble savages, both charming and exasperating.

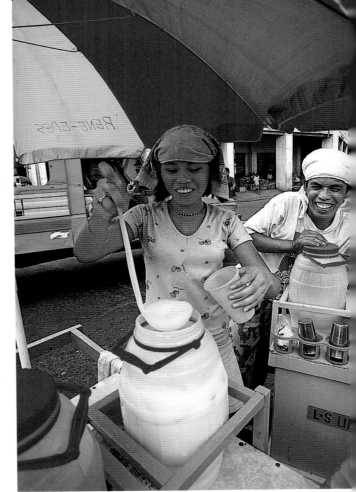

Left: A colorful Jeepney wends its way through traffic in Makati City. Passengers can hop on and hop off anytime.
Top: Smiling Davao girl with Mindanao dove.
Above: Proud Maranao women before a highborn household of Marawi City.
Right: A tricycle taxi, one of the most popular forms of local transport, in front of the Manila Cathedral in the Intramuros district of Manila.
Far right: Selling fresh *buko* juice at the Carbon Market in Cebu.

THE LEGACY of three centuries of Spanish colonization manifests itself among the oldest Catholic
churches of the country. From ancient San Agustin
Church with its carved doors and Chinese *fu* lions
to fine painted ceilings in medieval Intramuros to
Ilocandia up north, where the heavyset "earthquake
baroque" churches of Paoay, Santa Maria and Santa
Lucia stand.

While the family kinship system binds together
the country's 81 provinces, it is Catholicism, the
common religion and social glue, that underlines
the lifestyle—especially at fiesta time. Secular harvest
feasts merge with Christian worship as in the Feast of
the Santo Nino, and the Visayans celebrate dancing
fiestas such as the *Ati-Atihan* of Kalibo, *Sinulog* of
Cebu and *Dinagyang* of Iloilo. During Eastertime or
Holy Week, the island of Marinduque presents the
dramatic spectacle of the *Moriones* Festival, reenacting
the miraculous conversion of the Biblical legionnaire
Longinus. Quezon's *Pahiyas* or "Harvest Offering"
honors San Isidro de Labrador, patron saint of
farmers; homes are decorated with fruits of the
harvest and colored rice wafers called *kiping*.

Facing page: Mother Mary
prays for us near the Bantay
belltower of Vigan.
Left: Magellan's Cross planted
Catholicism in the center of
Cebu in 1517.
Below, left: Blessed is the
sleeping babe among the
Mama Marys and Santo Niños.
Below, right: Lighting votive
candles in a Baclaran church on
Wednesdays.
Bottom, left: Candlelit pro-
cession of "La Naval" from
Santo Domingo Church in
Quezon City.
Bottom, right: Stark and spare
San Joaquin Church in isolated
Batanes, northernmost islands
of the Philippines.

15

manila
by the bay

Manila began along the banks of the Pasig River, within Intramuros, the medieval Walled City. Today some twelve million urbanites jostle through Metro Manila, a chaotic, modern Asian metropolis.

t o touch the heart of old Manila, start with Rizal Park, Intramuros and Fort Santiago on the Pasig River—guardpost of the Spanish Walled City for three centuries. This medieval fortress with high walls contained the temporal and spiritual worlds, but few traces remain today beyond the stony gates. Visit the museums where Intramuros' memories are kept: Casa Manila near ancient San Agustin Church and the new Bahay Tsinoy (Chinese-Filipino) Museum. The creativity of the Filipinos is showcased in the Metropolitan Museum of Art, Coconut Palace and Cultural Center of the Philippines by the bayside.

Facing page, bottom: The Manila skyline at twilight, showing Bonafacio Global City, Ortigas.

This page, clockwise from below: The myriad of boats and yachts along Manila Bay, hotels in the background. An intact *baluarte* (balustraded fort) among the adobe walls of medieval Intramuros. Artists by the jeepney mural of Luneta.

ANILA'S FIRST HIGHRISE AREA is Makati, the modern satellite hub of big business, new ideas and progress. In Makati are classy hotels, upscale malls and East-West fusion cuisine restaurants; the financial district (Ayala Avenue); and elite residential villages. Everything is bigger, brighter and shinier in Makati, the new millennium side of Metro Manila.

Manila's big, circumferential highway is known affectionately as EDSA and has carried miraculous popular uprisings called "People Power." Together with the new Metro Railway Transit, EDSA links the major city hubs: Roxas Boulevard, rimming Manila

This page, clockwise from top: Manila's oldest church, San Augustin, has trompe l'oeil inside and a coral facelift outside. *Calesa* rides and cobblestones spell nostalgia near Casa Manila, Intramuros. An LRT train arrives at a station. The LRT serves 579,000 passengers each day. Its 31 stations are spread over 31 kilometers (19 mi) of mostly elevated track. Rizal Park by the bay with its flags, where Manila begins.

Facing page, clockwise: The famous Manila Bay sunset. Corregidor Island can be reached from Manila by hydrofoil. "The Rock" was made famous by the Allies' defence in 1942. Corregidor with its military installations and delightful scenery is a popular day-trip. The gateway to Fort Santiago, the military outpost guarding Manila for three centuries.

Bay to Makati with her spiffy Ayala Center; Ortigas Center in Pasig, the second largest business district in the country, where mega-sized shopping malls drive the consumer spirit; and Cubao in middle-class Quezon City, with its mass entertainment, music clubs and big university population.

Manila's urban sprawl is interknit by a massive case of Asian traffic—and colorful jeepneys. The virtual icon of Manila is the ubiquitous jeepney, that colorful chimera of public transportation that plies the city byways on short, zippy hauls. These multipassenger vehicles hark back to the days of American GI jeeps, even while they carry the cityfolk forward—with machismo—into the 21st century.

A popular escape from the madding crowd (and tourists' war memorial tour) is a foray to the Rock of Corregidor, the fortified island guarding Manila Bay. The Rock was the Allies' last bastion in the Pacific War. Today, visitors pay respects to the WW II gun battlements and underground tunnels where Filipino and American soldiers shared courage and history.

After the famous orange sunset on Manila Bay, night scenes light up the new yuppie entertainment area of Malate, behind the austere old Resurrection Church. Malate today means urban renewal on a charming scale: lots of stylish cosmopolitan cafés and crafts galleries cluster around Remedios Circle—like fireflies amid the night and music.

laguna & calabarzon

Just outside Manila lie five Tagalog provinces where one feels the pastoral rhythms of the country. "Calabarzon" encompasses Cavite, Laguna, Batangas, Rizal and Quezon.

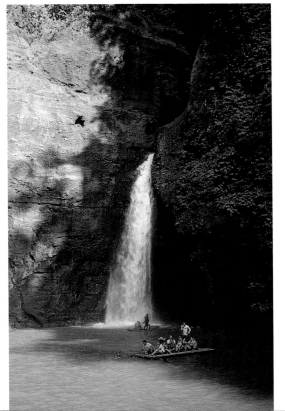

Laguna is a riverine province with a heart-shaped lake. Life here is cooler, wetter, more languorous. Rural forays will let you experience warm hospitality, local delicacies and the joys of rivers and springs. Refresh in the bubbly pools of Hidden Valley Springs. Ride the famous rapids of Pagsanjan River. Enjoy Villa Escudero on the border—a coconut plantation-cum-resort that offers day-trips to costumed nostalgia and watery picnics. Visit Taal, Batangas, with her huge basilica, see *balisong* knives and historic houses. Lucban and Sariaya towns in Quezon celebrate the charming *Pahiyas* Festival, when farmers decorate their homes with the harvest—fruit, vegetables and colored rice wafers called *kiping*.

Facing page, top: Waters from Villa Escudero's waterfall run through the picnic area.
Facing page, bottom: The Villa's cottages by the water —the coconut hacienda's own river.
This page, clockwise from top left: Pagsanjan's Shoot-the-Rapids ride is a memorable trip for visitors! Novel "Carabator" or carabao-drawn wagon tours the Villa's haciendas. Another weekenders' resort is popular Matabungkay Beach, Batangas. Pagsanjan River's source is the Magdapio waterfall, under which you will love to go rafting. *Pahiyas* Fiesta of Lucban, Quezon; homes are decorated with *kiping*.

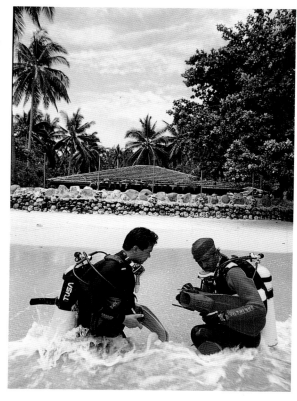

Clockwise from top left: Snorkeling in the clear waters of Hundred Islands, Pangasinan. The Bali Hai Resort in Bauang, La Union, on the west coast of Luzon. Taking scuba diving instruction at Dakak Resort, Dapitan, Zamboanga. Fishing near the Amanpulo Resort. Marine coral reefs from Batangas to Bohol offer seductive diving year-round. Guests' fleet of colorful sailing boats at Dakak Resort. **Facing page:** Windsurfing by a beach resort in Boracay.

vigan &
ilocandia

Ilocandia is a sparse and rugged land. Three northwestern provinces hug the northern coastline of Luzon—between the mountains and the sea—and harbor the cultural treasure known as Vigan.

Facing page: Old streets of Heritage village in Vigan; the tall stone mansions date back to 17th-century Chinese merchants.
Above: Boys and their goat in the warm Ilocos sunset.
Below: Paoay Church in Ilocos Sur is supported by thick stone buttresses—a unique style called "earthquake baroque."

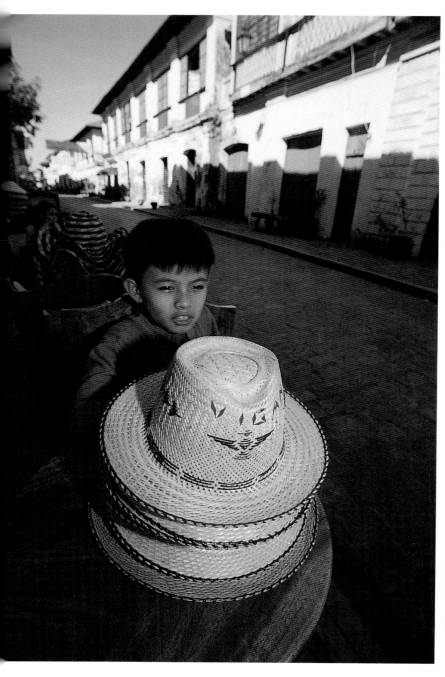

Clockwise from left: A boy of Ilocos sells Vigan souvenir cowboy hats made of woven bamboo. Vigan's traditional *burnayan* or pottery kiln makes pots in a giant wood-fired oven. *Molave* benches and old sugar mills on the sidewalk—part of the town's reproduction furniture trade. Venture north-ward and explore the cultural history museum of Laoag, Ilocos Norte. Cobbled streets among Vigan houses are a playground for kids with wheels.

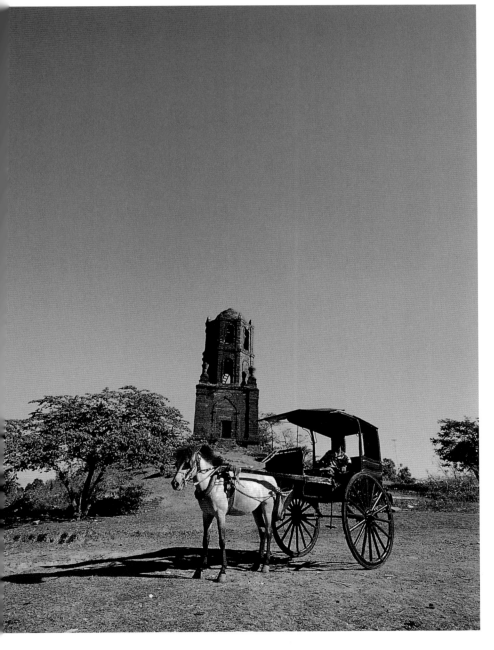

i LOCANDIA IS A RUGGED LAND comprising the northwestern provinces of La Union, Ilocos Sur and Norte where fields of tobacco, lone fishermen on dunelike shores and the finest highways of Luzon give Ilocandia a sparse, spare beauty. Vigan in Ilocos Sur is a heritage village stuck in time. It exudes an austere antiquity, especially the towering 18th-century mansions, all lined along cobblestone streets running straight and narrow between quarters. Visitors can view the elegant Quema mansion or stay in Villa Angela Heritage House, with its polished wooden floors, capiz windows and charm galore, or tarry at the old *burnayan*, the traditional pottery kiln.

Above, left: Old iron bridge over troubled waters, a landmark of hardy Ilocandia.
Above, right: Jesus Christ as a wood carving, on one of the streets of Vigan, Ilocos Sur.
Left: A low-slung *carretela* (horse carriage) of Vigan parks by the Bantay belltower.

Above: The Banaue rice terraces were hand-built by the Ifugaos over 2,000 years ago. **Facing page, top and bottom:** Treks around Ifugao and Bontoc expose visitors to the awesome sights of the highland. Five major tribal groups collectively known as Igorots live in the Cordillera.

baguio &

THE BANAUE RICE TERRACES in the Cordillera are the scenic highlight of Luzon. The grandeur of the rice terraces, along with the traditional lifestyle of the Ifugao tribespeople, make for a unique experience in the highlands. It's a hiker's mecca too. Ascend to the top and see the 100-sq-km range of terraces, carved by hand over 2,000 years ago. Wander Banaue town, or trek to Batad. Explore Sagada, the episcopal mission town in Bontoc, where coffins hang in great caves and massive limestone rocks mark the pathways. The awesome landscapes and ethnic traditions of the Cordillera create long-lasting impressions.

the cordillera

Behold the Banaue Rice Terraces and the hardy lifestyle of the Ifugao tribespeople for a unique experience of the Cordillera highlands.

BAGUIO CITY, the highland summer capital first established by the Americans in 1902, promises a springtime climate (20°C) and pine trees at 1,500 m above sea level. Baguio also means: a cowboy spirit among the cityfolk; horseback rides for tourists and evergreen attractions such as rollerskating and boating in Burnham Park; fresh strawberry jam and pink nuns. Baguio has the most colorful public market in the country—hanging with baskets, fruits, vegetables and golden, "everlasting" garlands. Baguio spells: schools and churches; golf courses and gardens; old-mine tours, cafés with fresh bread and serious coffee; plus a bazaar of souvenirs in silver and wood. The newest attraction is Tam-Awan, a recreated village of Igorot houses with art exhibits by indigenous artists.

This page, clockwise from left: Ifugao hut made of hardwood and thatch, in Tam-Awan Village, Baguio. The Flower Festival brings out the Kalinga costumes and Baguio beauties. Pony boys and horses in the morning mist of Wright Park in Baguio. Baguio has nurtured modern artwork from a guild of indigenous artists. Planting upland rice in a watery plot of Banaue in the Cordillera. Baguio's Burnham Park is a family place for leisure boating and biking. Facing page: In the mountain region of Sagada, people used to hang coffins with their dead on a cliff in Echo Valley, Northern Luzon.

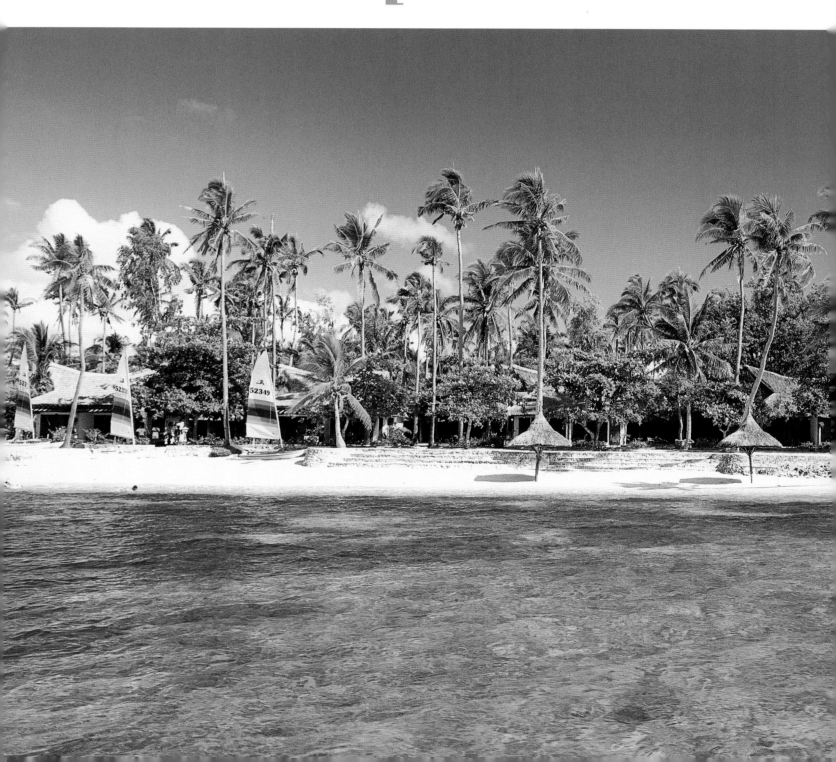

cebu & the visayan isles

Hanging midway down the archipel-ago like a necklace of uneven pearls, the Visayas comprise six major islands —Cebu, Bohol, Negros, Panay, Leyte and Samar—and their fringe isles.

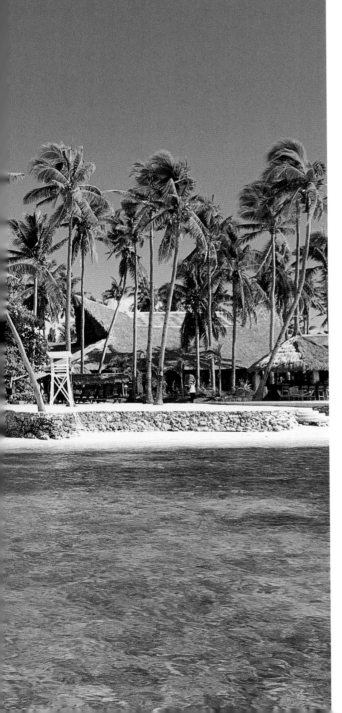

Facing page, top and bottom: A beach bunny in bikini on Mactan, Cebu's own resorts isle. The tropical resort formula: white sandy beach, aqua sea, palm trees and picturesque cottages —here those of Argao, Cebu.
Top: Basilica of Santo Niño in Cebu with the Sinulog parade.
Left: Relaxing in a resort on the island paradise of Panglao, down south of Bohol mainland.

V*IVE LA DIFFERENCE* of the Visayas: the slower pace of life; the seductive lilt of the languages; the loving women; the seafood, beaches, guitars; and the sweetest of mangoes. Cebu—Queen City of the South—was named the eighth most livable city in Asia! The Cebuanos work harder, try harder and have created the second biggest city in the country. Cebu boasts an international airport and malls and convention centers within this historical cradle of 16th-century Spanish Philippines.

bUSINESS-MINDED CEBU is a manufacturing
center and port, doing a thriving trade in
handicrafts and accessories, furniture and guitars.
Taste the seafood. Enjoy the nightlife. See
Magellan's Cross, the Basilica of the Santo Nino,
and Casa Gorordo for a glimpse of the city's
heritage. Catch Sinulog, Cebu's dancing, costumed
parade in January.

Iloilo possesses the gentility of a bygone era,
with its lovely ancestral houses of the Jaro district,
the folksy carvings on Iloilo's old churches and some
of the nicest people and pastries of the Visayas!
For adventure seekers, there's exotic Isla Naburot,
a private isle southwest of Guimaras Island. From
Iloilo, take a ferry to Bacolod in Negros, island of
the sugar barons and golfing center of the Visayas.
Here the Negrense people live hard, play hard and
enjoy the lifestyle of the modern *haciendero*. Both
creative crafts and wild notions originate here. Visit
Silay town to the north, with its ancestral mansions
and orchid farms. And be in Bacolod when the
stunning Masskara Festival unravels on the streets.

For scuba diving, plunge into the seas of Bohol,
southeast of Cebu, where rich fishing waters flow over
some of the Philippines' most seductive dive sites.

Facing page: Isla Naburot,
off Guimaras and Iloilo,
is a private isle made for
adventurous, Robinson
Crusoe-type guests.
**This page, clockwise from
left:** A resort cottage right by
the sea, for holiday-makers
in southern Cebu. Masskara
is a thanksgiving and Mardi
Gras—the ultimate costumed
revelry of Bacolod, Negros
Oriental. Mogambo Springs
at Plantation Bay Resort and
Spa on Mactan Island is a
fantasy resort built round a
shallow lagoon. Guitars are
a specialized product from
craftsy, musical Cebu.

boracay

Boracay, an island of white, flourlike sands and crystal-clear waters, has some of the best beaches in the world.

Left and above: Boracay has sleek *bancas* outriggers for island-hopping and photo opportunities everywhere.
Top: Peace and solitude and a shady hut on the wide, white Boracay shore.
Right: Boracay is considered the windsurfing capital of the Philippines.

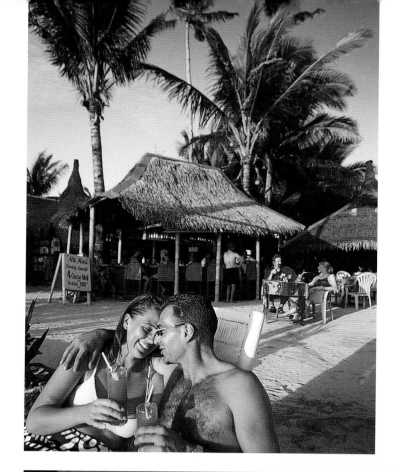

bORACAY, OFF AKLAN PROVINCE, is one long (7 km) beautiful white beach, regarded as one of the best beaches in the world, though it is lined by a hundred resorts—from long-stay budget rooms to high-end quarters in paradise. Beach culture has covered the entire island; today, 6,000 Boracay residents entertain some two million tourists a year. Both locals and foreigners flock to this faraway isle, for it is an exceptional confluence of pure, white flourlike sands and crystal-clear waters that ripple in the sun before turning turquoise over the depths. Boracay is one of the most enduring traveler's meccas.

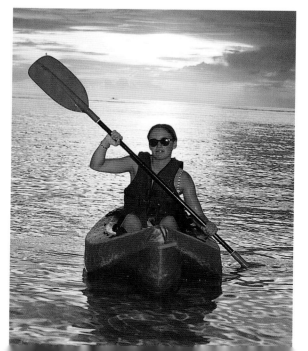

Top, left: Boracay T-shirts explode in the wild colors of the beach holiday.
Top, right: Sunset cocktails by the pool with jazz music, before Boracay's disco night takes over.
Middle, left: A golf course has arrived on Boracay.
Middle, right: Beach, beach and more beach.
Left: Sea kayaking, a meditative activity with the sea, has joined the resort isle's roster of waterborne sports.
Right: Fine white beach, golden girl and coconut palms in the breeze.

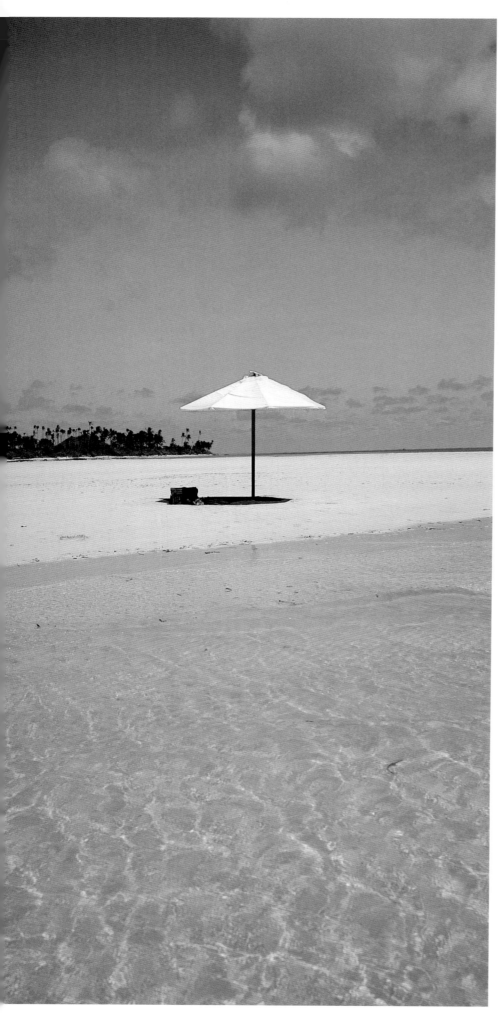

Hᴇᴀᴅ ᴛᴏ Nᴏʀᴛʜᴇʀɴ Pᴀʟᴀᴡᴀɴ for more exotic discoveries. Bacuit Bay abounds with spectacular nature spots, cathedral caves, marine gardens, black granite cliffs and pristine white sand beaches. All around soar dramatic landscapes of limestone, as well as unique marine seascapes.

Beyond the wonders of Nature, numerous chic boutique resorts have sprouted in the farthest reaches of Palawan. There are the El Nido Resorts, providing glamorous accommodations on stilts. Off sprawling Busuanga, there's Club Paradise, a favorite destination among expats, while nearby Calauit Nature Park harbors a selection of African savannah animals. Ensconced on the farthest outpost of Cuyo is Amanpulo, the boutique resort that is an icon of superstar luxury.

Facing page, clockwise from left: Pristine sands and crystal waters of the Cuyo Islands, site of Amanpulo. Calauit Island's Nature Park is home to giraffes, zebras and other African species. El Nido spells limestone caves cliffs and monoliths where gatherers climb to collect birds' nests for gourmet cuisine.

This page, clockwise from right: Club Noah-Isabelle in Taytay features cottages on stilts over water. Amanpulo's luxury casitas afford guests ultimate comfort and privacy. Coron Bay near Busuanga inspires fantastic sunsets and nature trips on land and water. Monkey walks the fiery Palawan sunset; the frontier land is wild and wondrous.

mindanao
—island of adventure

Mindanao, the largest island of the Southern Philippines, belongs to adventure travelers. Teeming with natural resources (along with a reputation for turbulence), Mindanao offers a tapestry of sights and experiences, from exotic flora and fauna to the fascinating cultures of tribal minorities.

MINDANAO, THE GREAT ISLAND south of the Visayas, is the Philippines' pioneer land, offering myriad experiences far from the madding urban crowd. Far-off Zamboanga on the northern edge of the Sulu Sea is the melting pot of the south, with five tribal minority groups coloring the cosmopolitan port town. Visitors can see the Muslim-influenced architecture of the Tausug, Yakan and Subanon among the churches, parks and botanical gardens. Just offshore, the stilt villages and boats of the Samal-Badjao people lend an exotic cachet, as Zamboanga sails onward under the image of sea gypsies' *vintas*—outrigger boats with multi-colored sails.

Facing page, top and bottom: Davao Mandaya family in tribal costumes. Aerial view of Dakak Resort, Zamboanga del Norte.
Top: Zamboanga girl on a colorful *vinta* of the Sulu Seas.
Middle, left: Clouds and mystery hover around Camiguin, an island of seven volcanoes.
Middle, right: Giant tuna harvest in General Santos, fishing port of Southern Mindanao.
Right: Volcanic Mt Hibok-Hibok as seen from the white island of Camiguin.

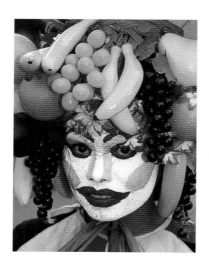

Right: A clown face among the festive fruits of Davao's Kadayawan Fiesta.

Below: A Mandaya weaver produces hemp cloth called *dagmay* on a backstrap loom.

Facing page, top to bottom: The Kadayawan Festival brings out the exotic costumes of the regional tribes. Davao's Apo View Hotel looks out over rolling golf links. Picturesque three-tiered gazebo and Samal-style cottages at the Pearl Farm.

Mindanao for the tourist often means Davao, the thriving industrial hub and province on the southeast quadrant. Davao City, one of the most expansive cities in the world, is big on exotic fruits, big on seafood and fish (exported through the port of General Santos), and big of heart for endangered species: in the foothills of Mt Apo (the country's highest peak) the Eagle Center breeds the endangered national bird, the Philippine Eagle. Davao is a sensual experience of orchid blooms (such as the vibrant *waling-waling)* and inimitable

durians; of religious shrines and mountain climbing
to the country's highest peak; of exotic fruit such as
marang, mangosteen, rambutan and *lanzones*; and
of *abaca* hemp weavings called *dagmay*, loomed by
the Mandayan tribespeople for tie-dyed, earth-toned
clothing and home decor. Davao is also the home of
the Kadayawan Festival, when the highly decorative
tribes of T'bolis and Bagobos converge and celebrate.

Mindanao welcomes sun and beach lovers. For
some, the picturesque designer resort Pearl Farm
on Samal Island south of Davao is reason enough
for venturing to Mindanao. The luckiest adventure
travelers have discovered Siargao town off Surigao
for its surfing and scenery, and Camiguin Island off
Cagayan de Oro for its natural hot and cold springs
and many volcanic splendors. Tiny, tear-shaped
Camiguin is an exceptionally beautiful isle of seven
volcanoes amid forested hills, rimmed by rolling
white sand beaches.

Above: An array of Filipino desserts on a banana leaf—rice patties with sesame and coconut, *Palitao* (left), brown rice cake, *Kutsinta* (middle) and cassava patties with coconut, *Pichi-Pichi* (right).

filipino food

Filipino food is a blend of Malay, Spanish and Chinese influences. Seafood, chicken and pork come in sauces of garlic, vinegar, soy, calamansi and coconut.

K*AIN NA!* LET'S EAT! A typical Filipino family meal begins with a variety of tropical fish and crustaceans and continues through a melange of basic spices—garlic, ginger, vinegar, soy sauce and calamansi (sweet baby limes). Seafood, chicken and pork are sautéed, stewed or roasted as main courses, while desserts are concocted with coconut milk, rice flour, sugar and lots of tropical fruits.

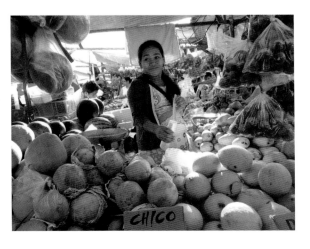

Facing page: A seafood buffet served up from Bacolod's seas. **Left:** A fruit vendor in the market in Cainta, Rizal. Fruits like these are popularly served during the New Year celebration. This is part of a Filipino tradition to welcome the New Year as it is believed to bring a whole year of good luck and abundance.

Right: Roast fish barbecue and coconut bowls make for a chic beach picnic in Palawan. **Facing page, clockwise from top left:** *Lechon* does a thriving business during celebrations. *Longganisa* are pork sausages, a specialty of select provinces. Fresh lobsters with a tranquil seaview of Samal Island. Exotic tropical fruits such as mangoes, durian and starfruit are exported from Cebu.

Above: Beef Kaldereta—with tomato sauce, carrots and potatoes—a popular dish in the Philippines, especially on Luzon Island.
Right: A beach restaurant on Boracay. This is a popular spot for tourist as you get to see the sunset and enjoy the food.

The *LECHON* or roast suckling pig—centerpiece of a Filipino fiesta—is roasted over coals till it's golden crispy and served with a sweet liver sauce. *Sinigang* is the local bouillabaisse, containing seafood or meat cooked in a mildly sour broth. *Adobo* is a popular chicken or pork dish, stewed with soy sauce, vinegar, garlic and peppercorns. Filipinos are blessed with an exotic variety of tropical fruit—from the incomparable Philippine mango to myriad bananas, pineapples, *atis*, *chico*, durian and mangosteen. Traveling foodies should also watch out for the varied regional cuisines offered at hotel buffets—especially the rich and tasty cooking from Pampanga, province of the best cooks.

music &
dance

Whether artist or artiste, folksy or fine, Filipinos are artful performers of unique caliber. In music, song and dance, they excel in the performing arts.

In the performing arts, the Filipino is a sheer adept and cultural accumulator. Especially in Western pop music: what was once local musicians' imitation of the American country-western sound has evolved into a movable feast of original Filipino music. Filipino bands now roam the nightclubs and hotels of Asia, and individual musicians have become the most versatile singing icons and serenaders of Asia, in three languages. Top billed pop performers such as Kuh Ledesma, Regine Velasquez and Gary Valenciano (with his superb dancing form) turn out rave musical productions unparalleled in the region.

Filipinos excel in dancing—on stage or on the street. Cities have their own ballet schools, folk dance groups and show troupes for television, promotions and special events. And of course, there is the public theater of the streets, unraveling in every town fiesta filled with costumed dancing parades.

Filipinos love everything showbiz and entertainment—it comes merged with American pop and national politics. Legitimate theater is alive and well in Manila's theater companies such as Repertory Philippines, based at Shaw Center, Ortigas, and the Filipino-language drama of the main theater of the Cultural Center of the Philippines. There is also Trumpets Playhouse and New Voice Theater for children's musicals and women's drama.

Facing page, top: Muslim dancer on an ancient wall.
Facing page, bottom: Feminine "flowers" dancing in Baguio's own Flower Festival in February.
Below: *Singkil* with fans, performed by a Bayanihan folk dancer.
Bottom: Bamboo Manalac in Bacolod City. A famous filipino musician and singer-songwriter, he began his career as the vocalist for Rivermaya and later fronted his own band, Bamboo.

ᴅance has also emerged as a fine art form. Several companies—Ballet Philippines, Philippine Ballet Theater and Ballet Manila—perform classical repertoires each season. Then there's BP's modern dance event, the "Neo-Filipino Series," which has been in performance for eight innovative years, presenting collaborations between the avant-garde and the classical arts, harnessing new music and video, as well as productions by creative designers. Neo-Filipino dance artistes with their stunning theaterpieces have been called counterpoint choreographers and sophisticated rebels.

Facing page, clockwise from top left: Bayanihan folk dancers make ready for the rural hat dance. A costumed Cebuana carries her Santo Niño in the Sinulog Festival. Grace Nono, small but stunning ethnic rock priestess, and the Pinikpikan band.

This page, clockwise from top left: An elder participates in the pagan-Christian Ati-Atihan Fiesta. A "Roman soldier" taking a musical break from the Moriones Festival in Marinduque. Cultural dancers perform in Pasinaya the Pasinaya Open House Festival in Manila—the largest multi-art presentation in the Philippines. The Ati-Atihan of Kalibo, Aklan, spawned a "generic" dance that is now performed everywhere.

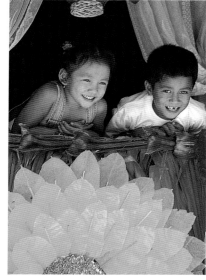

All roads lead through Manila, gateway to the islands. Holidays begin when Filipinos—displaying their famous hospitality—greet you with friendly smiles and hip English.

visiting
the philippines

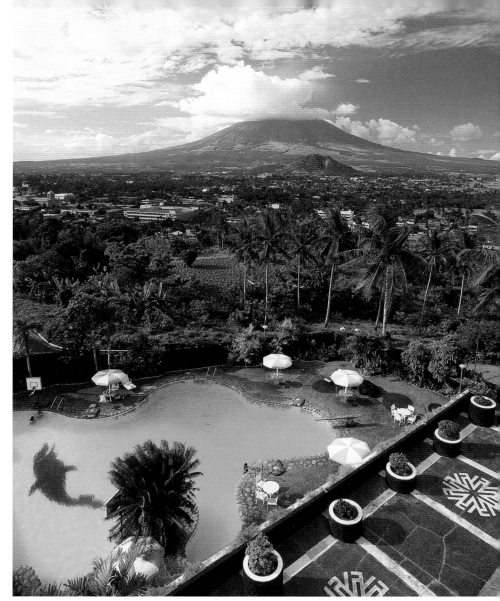

HE BEST TIME to visit the Philippines is from mid-October through February—after the rains, but before the hot summer months of April and May. The four festive months comprise the best time for beachgoing and touring; and January is a good time to catch the Visayas' dancing fiestas. Most visitors come to Manila by air, arriving at Ninoy Aquino International Airport or Cebu's Mactan International Airport (30 minutes from the beach). With some planning, one can spend a varied week on these shores, going on a city tour of Intramuros, Fort Santiago and Manila's new cultural museums; on day-trips to Pagsanjan Falls, Villa Escudero or Tagaytay Ridge; or island-hopping down to the resort beaches of Cebu or Boracay.

Facing page, top: Flower children at the Pahiyas Festival in Lucban, Quezon.
Facing page, bottom: Swimming pool and open thatched restaurant of the China Sea Resort in Bauang, La Union, on the West Coast of Luzon.
This page, clockwise from top: Swimming pool of the Mayon International Hotel in Legaspi City, with Mayon Volcano looming in the background. The Costa Aguada Resort on Guimaras spells provincial pleasures for families. Amanpulo resort casita on Cuyo Island stands for six-star luxury in the utmost privacy. Mountain bikes for an island-hopping excursion, Boracay.

Above: Boracay beach.
Front cover and flap: The beautiful lagoon on the island of Coron, Palawan. Diving at Apo Island.
Back cover: Pampanga volcano and rice paddies.

Published by Tuttle Publishing, an imprint of Periplus Editions (HK) Ltd

www.tuttlepublishing.com

Copyright © 2016 Periplus Editions (HK) Ltd

All rights reserved. No part of this publication may be reproduced or transmitted in any form or by any means, electronic or mechanical, including photocopy, recording or any information storage and retrieval system, without prior written permission from the publisher.

ISBN 978-0-8048-4624-0

Distributors:

North America, Latin America & Europe
Tuttle Publishing
364 Innovation Drive
North Clarendon, VT 05759-9436
Tel: 1 (802) 773-8930
Fax: 1 (802) 526-2778
info@tuttlepublishing.com
www.tuttlepublishing.com

Japan
Tuttle Publishing
Yaekari Building, 3rd Floor
5-4-12 Osaki, Shinagawa-ku
Tokyo 141-0032
Tel: (81) 3 5437-0171
Fax: (81) 3 5437-0755
tuttle-sales@gol.com

Asia Pacific
Berkeley Books Pte. Ltd.
3 Kallang Sector #04-01
Singapore 349278
Tel: (65) 6741 2178
Fax: (65) 6741 2179
inquiries@periplus.com.sg
www.tuttlepublishing.com

24 23 22 21
7 6 5 4 3

Printed in China   2107EP

TUTTLE PUBLISHING® is a registered trademark of Tuttle Publishing, a division of Periplus Editions (HK) Ltd.

PHOTOGRAPHIC CREDITS

Beck, Joseph (Photobank Singapore), pp. 5 (top), 45 (bottom left). **Beiboer, Paul,** pp. 35 (middle left). **Bautista, Bien S.,** pp. 4, 7 (middle right), 13 (top), 14, 15 (top), 19 (top), 20 (top), 21 (middle left), 23 (top left, middle left, middle right and bottom), 24 (bottom), 35 (top left, top right and bottom right), 46 (left and top right), 47 (top left), 49 (middle right), 53 (top center and middle right), 61 (bottom). **Davocol, Emil V.,** pp. 2, 7 (bottom), 11 (top), 12, 18 (top, middle left and middle right), 22 (bottom), 24 (top), 26 (bottom left), 27, 28, 29, 30 (top left, middle right and bottom left), 31 (top left and bottom), 32, 33 (bottom), 35 (middle right), 36 (bottom), 39 (top right), 41 (top and bottom), 42 (middle right), 48 (top), 49 (middle left), 50, 51 (top and bottom), 52, 53 (top left), 54, 57 (top left and top right), 58 (bottom), 62 (top). **Garbutt, Veronica,** pp. 15 (bottom right), 19 (bottom right), 22 (top), 23 (top right), 26 (top right, middle left and middle right), 46 (bottom right), 57 (bottom left and bottom right), 62 (bottom), 63 (top). **Heaton, Dallas & John (Photobank Singapore),** pp. 39 (top left). **Jezierski, Ingo,** pp. 36 (top), 64. **Lucero, Patrick Nagaishi,** back cover (middle left), pp. 7 (top and middle left), 9, 11 (middle right), 13 (bottom), 15 (middle left and bottom left), 25 (top), 26 (top left and bottom right), 30 (top right and bottom right), 31 (top right), 33 (top), 35 (bottom left), 37 (top), 39 (bottom), 42 (top left, top right, middle left and bottom), 45 (top and bottom right), 47 (top right and bottom), 49 (bottom), 49 (top), 51 (middle), 53 (middle left), 60 (top right), 61 (top left, top right), 63 (top left and bottom left). **Montifar, Raul M.,** pp 44. **Simmons, Ben (Photobank Singapore),** p. 11 (middle left). **Tapan, George,** pp. 17 (top), 37 (bottom). **Tettoni, Luca Invernizzi (Photobank Singapore),** pp. 17 (bottom left and bottom right), 21 (top and middle right), 38, 47 (middle right), 53 (top right), 55 (top), 56 (top), 59 (top), 60 (top left and bottom). **Vidler, Steve (Photobank Singapore),** pp. 5 (bottom), 19 (bottom left), 43. **Wassman, Bill (Photobank Singapore),** pp. 58 (top). **Yabao, Sonny,** pp. 20 (bottom), 21 (bottom), 48 (bottom), 63 (bottom right). **Stock Photos,** (front cover): ID 192330044 © saiko3p | Shutterstock.com; (front cover flap): ID 182300069 © soft_light | Shutterstock.com; (back cover): ID 3025102 © simongurney | iStockphoto.com; (cover spine): ID 51745614 © tropicalpixsingapore | iStockphoto.com; (endpapers): ID 10078482 © Dowhup | Dreamstime.com; pp. 1: ID 6106501004394496 Festival in the Philippines © Michael Ash | Pixoto.com; pp. 6: ID 44893999 © Agaliza | Dreamstime.com; pp. 8 (above): ID 233825812 © View Apart | Shutterstock.com; pp. 8 (below): ID 173765885 © View Apart | Shutterstock.com; pp. 10: ID 21400351 © Holger Mette | iStockphoto.com; pp. 11, (bottom): ID 140062801 © Tappasan Phurisamrit | Shutterstock.com; pp. 16 (above): ID 43624897 © JS | fotolia.com; pp. 16 (below): ID 67677401 © Holger Mette | iStockphoto.com; pp. 18: ID 20008038 © joyt | iStockphoto.com; pp. 34: ID 50299184 © Florian Blümm | Dreamstime.com; pp. 39 (middle right): © Mogambo Springs at Plantation Bay Resort and Spa | plantationbay.com; pp. 41 (middle left): ID 116003776 © leoks | Shutterstock.com; pp. 53, (bottom): ID 5203844628217856 The Potter © Jimmy Hilario | Pixoto.com; pp. 54 (bottom): ID 36341968 © Junpinzon | Dreamstime.com; 56 (middle left): ID 28749893 © Alexander Mychko | 123rf.com; pp. 56, (bottom right): ID 23013748 © Vojtech Vlk | Dreamstime.com; pp. 59 (bottom): ID 6178224639836160 Bamboo Manalac Concert © Joselito Labrador Jr. | Pixoto.com; pp. 61 (middle right): ID 38967526 © Antonio Magdaraog | Dreamstime.com

"Books to Span the East and West"

Tuttle Publishing was founded in 1832 in the small New England town of Rutland, Vermont [USA]. Our core values remain as strong today as they were then—to publish best-in-class books which bring people together one page at a time. In 1948, we established a publishing office in Japan—and Tuttle is now a leader in publishing English-language books about the arts, languages and cultures of Asia. The world has become a much smaller place today and Asia's economic and cultural influence has grown. Yet the need for meaningful dialogue and information about this diverse region has never been greater. Over the past seven decades, Tuttle has published thousands of books on subjects ranging from martial arts and paper crafts to language learning and literature—and our talented authors, illustrators, designers and photographers have won many prestigious awards. We welcome you to explore the wealth of information available on Asia at **www.tuttlepublishing.com**.